Corporate Lunacy

Behind the Scenes of

America's Worst Gas Station

Revised Edition

By Rob Clooney

Copyright by Rob Clooney, 2018; Revised edition, 2019

All rights reserved. This book, or parts thereof, may not be reproduced in any form without permission of the author.

This story is based on actual events, although the name of individuals and companies has been changed; exceptions made to verifiable wrestling related content. Any resemblance to identification of actual persons, living or dead, is entirely coincidental.

Any concerns about the legitimacy of these events can be verified by, but not limited to, various means of text messaging, emails, and testimonials.

Follow Rob Clooney at

www.facebook.com/AuthorRobClooney

www.twitter.com/clooney_rob

ISBN 978-0-359-68620-9

Preface

When I decided to take a trip to the 2018 U.S. Beach Wrestling National Championships, I decided on a road trip. Okay, to be fair, I hadn't considered flying from Michigan to North Carolina, a costly mistake I won't make again. I was so accustomed to being a "road warrior", driving throughout my wrestling career. My wrestling trip served a few purposes. Nearing 40 years of age, I wanted to test my abilities and see if I still had it. As someone who tries to promote the style of sand wrestling, it was a great networking experience behind the scenes. And for someone who loved their job as a general manager for the chain of "Slowway" convenience stores, it was a way to benchmark my store to dozens of other Slowway locations throughout 5 other states.

If you would have told me in May, while making the trek through the mountains on my way to the mid-Atlantic, that by the end of the year I would have a book cracking the top 10 lists on Amazon, I might have believed you. Heck, it might have given me a burst of motivation to hammer out one of the two books I was trying to get published by the end of the year.

If you would have told me this chart-topping book would be about calling out my employer for needlessly abusing a hardworking employee, I would have given you a look of disbelief. I loved my job and the family-like bond I shared with the crew. I had high aspirations to continuing climbing the corporate ladder alongside my wife. It was known to my supervisors during performance reviews I was interested in a spot as a monthly inspector, a position I would have been a natural for. The chances of me writing a book about Slowway were nil.

Now I'm reflecting in front of my laptop, one year later. *Corporate Lunacy* was published near the end of September, although promoting the book didn't begin until after my wife found another job in November. Honestly, I didn't expect much out of it, a market for this book may not exist. For me, it was therapeutic to write my version of events after being burned so badly.

It unexpectedly sold well, with word quickly spreading throughout the company. Many have expressed gratitude, there was finally a voice standing up for the overloaded store-level employees. It's unfortunate so many workers feel undervalued, and possibly the leading factor to *Corporate Lunacy* consistently performing in the top 10% on Amazon since November. As I write this, the paperback copy is performing in the top 1%.

This is a revised edition of *Corporate Lunacy*. The few spelling and grammar errors are fixed, and a few sentences are clarified. Nothing was deleted and the only added content is a new chapter to serve as the true ending of *Corporate Lunacy*, covering events after the first edition went to publication.

Not that I couldn't have added more information. I totally forgot to mention my wife was the winner of our district's "Manager of the Year" award at the symposium in chapter 9. I'd later learn the general manager fired from Chesterfield in chapter 2 was another instance of Jack throwing his managers under the bus, authorizing those overages of hours and then denying it afterwards. I failed to mention the Fraser location was one of dozens who lost air conditioning during a local heatwave, with temperatures exceeding 105 degrees inside the stores; the high temps caused our equipment to malfunction and it's been said employees from other locations were hospitalized, yet we were ordered to stay open. I could go on, but at this point I don't want to risk altering the aura of my story by altering any of its content.

I appreciate the overwhelming support, and hope you enjoy this rendition of *Corporate Lunacy; Behind the Scenes of America's Worst Gas Station*. I'm very sympathetic to the many who have experience similar situations. Let's hope these voices are heard and the corporate heads of Slowway begin appreciating their employees who actually interact with the customers inside their stores.

Thank you all,

Rob Clooney

Chapter 1

The winter of 2015-16 was a transitional one for this All World wrestler. I lost my job as a personal healthcare assistant, for reasons I can't divulge due to HIPPA laws, and was looking for work. My sporadic appearances as an independent professional wrestler helped earn a little side money but certainly not enough to pay the bills. The same held true for the few books I've published. I was set to start hosting sand wrestling tournaments in the summer, but not only was that months away, it required a bit of investing as well.

I had the opportunity to rejoin the ranks of Tacoland just weeks into my job search, a company I previously worked for during my teens and into early adulthood. I've always been fond of my memories with the company. So much so, that one of my pro wrestling personas I still use on occasion is the character named Taco Man, a masked fast food worker who hides his identity so his boss doesn't find out he took off to wrestle during his smoke break. It's just an enhancement character, meant to give newer wrestlers an easy win just before they're victimized by a shattering plastic serving tray. Tacoland provided me with my first managerial experiences, having held the title of shift leader for a number of years before considered for a promotion to assistant manager. I was optimistic about returning to Tacoland, even if it has been over 15 years since I've worked for the company.

Before being hired, I had interviews with two general managers, both of whom saw me as management material. It was decided between them I would work at the franchise location in

Richmond, Michigan, as the location was in more need for experienced help than the store in Macomb. I was open to the idea of management, but wanted a flexible schedule so I could keep my sand wrestling tournament commitments. Many of these tournaments were geared towards the local communities, with a pair of major tournaments, one of which was a National Championship for the State Games of America. Besides, if I held off from being a manager until the end of the summer may have been more respectful among my coworkers instead of potentially jumping in front of someone else who deserved a promotion.

My enthusiasm continued until the end of my training period. I realized afterwards anyone who wasn't a manager was stuck fighting for hours as part time employees. I'm unsure if it was simply the current business model or if the Affordable Healthcare Act had an influence, but I took it personally. If I was a part time employee, was my experience really needed at this location? I went to the general manager in Macomb and inquired about transferring to her store, but by then their staffing needs were met. But looking back at this very paragraph, it would've probably been a part time position there as well unless I made the jump to a manager.

I wasn't necessarily stressed. I was still collecting unemployment benefits from the care giving position, with my Tacoland wages deducted from those benefits. I kept busy writing, working on an updated version of *Hosting Beach Wrestling Events* and tinkered a bit with a memoir with the working title *A Solid Performance*. I mostly focused my literary efforts on a fictional story I've had dancing around in my head for several years, and thought it was publisher-ready. But it wasn't as it was rushed, and a manuscript I'm still working on (working title *Fast Cash*). The reason for rushing it was because unemployment was only going to lend a helping hand for so long and part time hours just wasn't enough.

A number of employees were great to work alongside, but some of the more experienced members seemed to always give me a bad attitude. When the crew realized I've previously worked at Tacoland, I think some of these coworkers felt threatened I might be given a managerial opportunity before they would. It didn't matter I've openly talked about hosting tournaments in the summer and wouldn't have a flexible availability required for the position. Whatever, I wasn't going to allow myself to get tangled within their web of gossip.

While I didn't recognize it right away, the ring leader of this clique was the assistant manager. While she was a hard worker, she lacked any accountability and played favorites. Another member of this clique was her daughter. Come on now, you can't have a supervisor position and be fair to your crew if one of those crew members is your child. The daughter was next in line for a chance at becoming a shift leader and certainly one who felt threatened by my presence. While she did the job well, she treated members of the crew just as her mother did, play favorites with the clique and treat everyone else poorly.

Here's an example of the assistant manager's lack of accountability. She often worked on the assembly line, starting the orders before sliding these Mexican-inspired food products to the "stuffer" to fill and wrap. The assistant manager would miss an item from the order about every 15-20 items she made, and instead of just making the missing item she would shift the blame to the stuffer for handing out that item in the previous order. She would yell and make a scene, unless you were a member of her inner circle. Then it was akin to, "It's okay, just pay more attention next time."

On three separate occasions, I was the stuffer while the assistant manager was responsible for starting the food preparation. I always took the berating the first time and followed up by slowing down. By slowing down, I was able to point out to her and the crew that it was indeed her fault for the missing item. I became more vocalized after it happened the second time, "No, you didn't make it." Then I would get booted from working on the line with her. After this cycle happened the third time, she never let me work alongside her again, possibly fearful I could do her job better than she could. If that's what she thought, she would be right. She wasn't accustomed to being called out on her mistakes.

Right next door to Tacoland was a Slowway gas station I frequently visited. It was a great group of workers, my favorite being my future-wife, who I was already dating and lived with. I griped to the team at Slowway about the assistant manager on a few occasions and let it be known I was looking for another job. I believe it was Jerome, the general manager at Slowway, who gave me the idea of applying at Slowway. I certainly didn't have a reason not to and filled out a job application for a shift lead position the very same day.

A few days went by and I was told the Slowway district manager, Jack Dickenwetter, wanted to meet me for an interview at the Richmond location. Jack must have been impressed with my resume because I didn't believe he normally came out to the stores to conduct interviews. I'm confident I passed Jack's inquiries with flying colors as he seemed to stumble a bit to find situational questions to truly round out the interview process. My only setbacks were disclosing an injury I've previously had in my wrist, but assured him I could work without any issues. And there was the DUI I had few years prior but completed my lawful punishment and had a valid driver's license. I'm not going to get into details about the injury, as doesn't fit the narrative of this story, but a wrestling related injury I certainly cover in my upcoming memoir.

I knew the DUI would slow down my background check and continued to work at Tacoland during the wait. On one eventful day working at Tacoland, we seemed a bit short staffed. I was on the inside register and the mother and daughter duo worked the line while a high school student ran the drive through window. The assistant was trying to expedite her daughter's shift lead training, and did so in a questionable way. She only opened one line instead of the customary two, preventing me from helping with the simple orders whenever the inside was slow. I'm just watching the times of these orders gradually increase as the lunch rush marched on, and at times said these orders were placed 30 minutes ago. It didn't matter to the related duo, as they wanted to do it by themselves.

Near the end of the assistant manager's shift, I directly told her what I thought of her as the next shift came in for the evening shift. "You're a shitty manager," followed by telling her and the oncoming manager I'm taking my break. I wasn't asking for a break, I just head out the door and ignored her ticked off squawking. As intended, I came back 30 minutes later.

The timing was right because I heard from Slowway that I was hired. I asked Jack to allow me to finish my schedule with Tacoland, which he seemed to respect. The pressure from the clique only thickened after calling out their ringleader, but I expected as much. I found out during my final week at Tacoland the general manager was under the impression I changed my mind about being a manager with their company. Hmm, I wonder who put that in his head. It's not as if she respected him either, overhearing the clique talk behind the general manager's back that the assistant was more qualified than he was to run the store. No, she wasn't.

In the end, at least I had a new updated outfit for Taco Man.

My first day on the job with Slowway was Friday, March 11th, 2016. As with most new jobs, the first day was focused on training. The training program for the shift lead position lasted a few months with a mix of training videos, workbooks, classes and hands-on experience. The initial day of training was going smoothly for the first few hours, until the store was surprised by their monthly inspection, which I will cover in greater detail later in this story. It can be stressful for managers as their paychecks were directly affected on how well they performed during these mystery shops.

Not long after the store inspection started, Jack showed up to the store with his boss, Mac Mooron, the Regional Manager. While there were other things Jack and Mac wanted to discuss with Jerome, one reason for the visit was so Jack could introduce me to Mac. Jack was bragging to Mac about finding a quality employee with plenty of management experience in the fast food sector. During my conversation with the district and regional manager, they keyed me in that the company was investing a large amount of resources in the food sector in an attempt to compete in the fast food market. They sure made me feel I could be a major asset to help Slowway accomplish this goal. I was just as confident they made the right decision hiring me with that objective in mind.

Jack and Mac also wanted to discuss various topics with Jarome, who was also preoccupied with the monthly inspection. "Sorry, Rob. There's just too much going on today to train you so why don't you go home and we'll get a fresh start on Monday." I certainly understood. It was the final week I would claim unemployment benefits, so I wasn't losing any money. I was full of optimism all over again after meeting Mac, even more excited than I was with idea of returning to Tacoland a few months prior. All three managers certainly left me with the feeling that I was their new, shiny penny.

Chapter 2

After just a few weeks of working at Slowway, I was requested to fill in at the location in Marysville. My managerial training was maybe a quarter complete but the higher ups had the upmost confidence in the abilities of their shiny new penny. The store needed coverage while the general manager took an out-of-state vacation. I accepted the challenge as I wanted to demonstrate I was a team player, despite a much longer commute. The shift lead in Marysville would essentially be the one in charge while I would become her temporary shift lead during a 10-day span.

I didn't think much of the request; I was just going to fill in and return to Richmond to continue my training. My peers at my location thought otherwise. While filling in for a store wasn't uncommon, helping out another district was supposedly a big deal. Marysville wasn't just outside the district, but a southern store in the neighboring region. District and regional managers wouldn't send someone to another region if they didn't believe their lent employee would excel, as they put their reputation on the line. To send an employee to provide coverage for a vacationing general manager would only improve their image to their supervisors, the same way my willingness to help improved my image with Jack and Mac.

The store was slightly bigger than Richmond, but still one of the company's smaller outlets. The crew was welcoming and I'm sure my ability to keep busy helped. I had a firm grasp on the duties of a crew member, completing the daily tasks assigned in a monthly workbook and labeled a natural on the register. I had a great knack at suggestive selling, having won numerous awards for my grasp on upselling psychology during those early Tacoland days. I've also had plenty of janitorial experience and constantly looked for something to clean when all other tasks were completed. The only piece of equipment I was unfamiliar with was the frozen coffee machine but didn't need to worry about it, since the frozen coffee machine was only cleaned twice a month.

My managerial skills were certainly tested as I was the least experienced employee during my temporary tenure at Marysville. Most of my teachings were instructional and this was my first crack at a hands-on approach. I didn't have the luxury of receiving any feedback or guidance, just left to venture on my own. In fact, I was working alone during my shifts whenever I was in charge of completing the paperwork so I could only get to the computer between customers. Looking back, I know I've botched the daily reports but I also know my simple mistakes were easily fixable.

I had the feeling the Marysville crew was told I worked for Slowway longer than I actually had. Not doing the daily paperwork properly and tackling the tasks instead of delegating responsibilities gave them an impression I was unqualified to be a shift leader but a capable crew member. Midway through my stint, I was open about my first day at Marysville being maybe my 13th shift with the company. I actually thought they were aware I was still early in my training but they weren't. After they knew, I'd like to believe I won the crew over before my final shift outside the region…at least a little.

There was still much to learn about Slowway, but I quickly realized the demands of the position prevented me from properly hosting any sand wrestling tournaments. It was the same fear I had with Tacoland, but I had to think about my family. I cancelled all thoughts of running any events and turned the State Game tournaments over to another club. I would still offer to help tournaments whenever I could, as I'd done the previous year with the inaugural Michigan Beach Wrestling Series. Helping would be a silver lining of sorts, disappointed with my inability to host any of my own.

There wasn't any rush to complete my training after I returned to Richmond. The idea within the store was Sabrina, the current shift lead, didn't really want to be a manger. She only agreed to take the promotion so my future wife, the longtime former shift lead, would be able to take a promotion to assistant manager at another store (and by this time, my wife cruised through her training and was already given a general manager position). The plan between me, Sabrina, and Jerome was she would step down after my training period was completed and I would step into the store's shift lead position. With that mindset, we had all the time in the world to work on the finer details of the managerial position.

Jack didn't get the message, nor did he approve. He had bigger plans and shipped me out to the Slowway in nearby Chesterfield, a much bigger and busier location. There was an overhaul in Chesterfield as the general manager was terminated for manipulating the designation of her crew's worked hours. The company doesn't honestly allow for enough man-hours to adequately operate their stores to their high level of expectations, a consequence of upper management making decisions without ever having worked inside these stores. A 4-year college degree is a prerequisite for a non-store management position and the company seemed to overvalue these degrees instead of considering anyone's work experience. Some of these degrees were unrelated to retail, such as photography.

This terminated GM thought she found a way to beat the system. After submitting payroll, the GM would go back and reassign these hours as "training hours", which do not count against the store. She went over by at least 100 hours per week and heard it could've been closer to 200. I have no idea how long this was going on but corporate is inevitably going to find out and they did. Not only did the GM lose her job but the shift lead was either terminated or quit. There wasn't a complete overhaul, as the assistant manager and other crew members kept their positions.

The incoming GM was Maggie, a longtime employee who worked her way up from being a crew member. Maggie started working in the district but was moved to another district and this was her opportunity to return to our district. I was brought in the day after she was. Maggie was expecting a strong shift leader who was highly touted by Jack, someone who could help while she scrambled to figure out the strengths and weaknesses of the Chesterfield crew.

What Maggie really got was a shift leader behind in his training. While I had started to get most of the technicalities down, I wasn't exactly the most efficient at getting certain things done within time constraints. My lack of strengths in the managerial position didn't make Maggie's position any easier and I think she tried to get me transferred for a more experienced shift leader. There was more to learn at Chesterfield, my first time working at a store that offered pizza and freshly made sandwiches. I was excited to finally be working with food and confident I could learn everything within a few hours of training based on my previous food experiences, which weren't limited to Tacoland by the way.

Maggie didn't have time to train me with the food but assured me she would. At that moment, there were understandably other priorities to tackle. Not only was she busy learning the skill set of the crew, there was a lot of neglected tasks desperately needing attention. The crew as a whole wasn't used to working with 25%-50% reduction in manpower, so they were asked to step up their game and not everyone could. The part time employees were getting fewer hours so their paychecks were slashed. These issues were not a great combination for the team's moral.

My moral wasn't great either. I was stuck on afternoons and couldn't get any other shifts. Basically, Maggie worked in the mornings and the assistant worked the morning whenever Maggie was off and the afternoons when she wasn't. I was the lowest manager on the totem pole so I was stuck in the afternoon time slot when the assistant wasn't. With my fiancé and kids busy in the mornings and asleep after I came home, I never spent time with my family. While I needed income to help support them, I wasn't willing to sacrifice spending time with them for a job. I was usually called in during my off days too, being told I didn't have the option not to come in since I was a manger.

These shifts at Chesterfield could be brutal. I was usually left alone during the end of shifts. No matter how presentable the store looked it never stayed that way a few hours later when the overnighter started their shift. That's if and when an overnighter came in at all. On a few occasions, I had to work the entire evening shift by myself whenever my only scheduled coworker either called off or just didn't bother to show up at all. I was always working past my scheduled time to smooth the shift transition or because I was stuck there.

Maggie was not a fan of me staying late to help, stressing the importance of working within the hours scheduled. I've received numerous verbal warnings on the matter but leaving a mess for the next person was just something I couldn't bring myself to do. Working at the Chesterfield location convinced me Slowway wasn't the right fit for me or my family so I began searching for something else.

There was a part of me determined to prove my worth, despite psychologically throwing in the towel. I came in one afternoon just before Maggie and the assistant were about to stock the cooler. It typically took the two of them a little more than 2 hours. I asked them if I could take a crack at it. "Be my guest," Maggie snickered. I came out of the cooler 50 minutes later and Maggie asked, "Did you need some help back there?" She didn't believe me when I told her I was finished and headed back to verify my work. Reading her silent lips when she came back out said it all, "Wholly shit!"

Impressing Maggie gave me a much-needed boost to my confidence and I started working harder for my GM, despite being set on finding employment elsewhere. I've thoroughly cleaned out the outside trash cans, removing the horrid vomit smell. I always picked up trash around the parking lot whenever I stepped out for a cigarette (I know, I know. I'm a wrestler who smokes. I've heard it a million times before). She eased up a bit when I worked beyond my shift, because she knew I was working hard whenever I was on the clock.

Mac Mooron was set to visit the store to see how we were doing. The store was still neglected in many areas, very dirty and plenty of expired items sitting on the shelves. I had the opportunity to run around and take care of these issues with the help of a seasoned cashier holding her own on the registers. I tackled months of neglect in the matter of 8 hours. Maggie didn't ask me too, nor was it expected.

When I came in the following afternoon, Maggie was standing behind a register without any customers. She looked at me as I walked through the door with a glowing smile, "Thanks, Rob." Apparently, Mac was thoroughly impressed and stated it was the cleanest he has ever seen that store. I made her look like a rock star to our regional manager and she certainly showed appreciation for my efforts. While I may not have been the strongest asset with paperwork and such, I certainly proved my worth.

On a rare moment my fiancé and myself had the same day off, we were out and about when I received a phone call from Maggie. Sabrina had successfully petition Jack to step down from the shift lead position in Richmond. I was given the option to either stay at the Chesterfield store or return to Richmond. I choose to go back to Richmond. Now I wouldn't be stuck on afternoons and could spend quality time with my family. I felt Maggie really wanted me to stay on her crew. That certainly wasn't the case when I first met her just one month prior.

To make room for my return, Sabrina was transferred to another location. The company already invested in her training and unwilling to designate her back to a crew member. The compromise was to make her a food steward at one of the stores that offered freshly cooked items, a step somewhere between a crew member and a shift leader. I had some big shoes to fill. Sabrina had a few years with the company and a favorite among the regular customers in Richmond. But I was confident I could fill those shoes just fine, even if I needed to break them in a bit.

In less than a week after my return to Richmond, Jerome had issues which placed him on medical leave. All of a sudden, I'm in charge of the store. I hadn't developed any more training on the paperwork aspect, possibly rusty since I hadn't done some aspects since leaving Richmond. This penny was now left to either sink or swim. I don't about you, but I've never seen any pennies float to the top of a wishing well.

Chapter 3

So I was left in charge of running the daily operations in Richmond despite not fully completing my shift leader training. It didn't take me long to knock off any rust this penny developed in Chesterfield, since the responsibilities of the managerial team rest solely on my shoulders. I'm grateful I had an experienced team around me, as it certainly alleviated the pressure of having the temporary duties of the general manager position. I also had the support of other general managers within the district I could turn to and Jerome was readily available for guidance.

My biggest supporter was my fiancé. I've already mentioned she worked at this Richmond location and knew the ins-and-outs better than anyone I turned to. I constantly picked her brain, not only at work but at home too. She knew the strengths and weaknesses of the crew, offering guidance on how to best utilize the staff's abilities. Don't get me wrong, Jerome started my training and there's plenty I learned by making mistakes. But if you were to ask me who my trainer was, I would have to honestly say it was my fiancé.

Whenever I was in doubt and couldn't call upon someone for help, I asked myself, "What would I do if I owned this business?" I've had a few unsuccessful attempts at business ownership, both in the profit and nonprofit sectors. Although these previous ventures didn't work out, I certainly learned from them. I surprised myself on my ability to make quick decisions based on these experiences, even though they were in sports and fitness instead of retail. It might've helped my abilities for my crew to treat me as the leader of the team, which they certainly did.

None of the help I had or reverting from previous experiences alleviated the pressure of working every day. Slowway required managers to work at the stores for a set number of hours, which varied based on the store's size. This requirement was every day. I wasn't offered any managerial help from Jack. In fact, I hadn't seen or heard from Jack after Jerome went out on medical leave. Jack really left me on my own and I had no work-life balance, despite the work-life balance being a theme the company pretended to boast.

As the summer marched on, being forced to work every day meant I couldn't help the Beach Wrestling Series. The idea of helping was my silver-lining when I abandoned the idea of running my own tournaments, and that wasn't happening. There's an unwritten rule in amateur sports if you reach a certain level of success, you should give back to the sport. I was disheartened every time I was stuck at the store in Richmond while a tournament was going on somewhere in the mitten. While my crew and others within the district kept telling me how great I was doing, I felt like a complete failure.

During this summertime stretch, the store had two monthly inspections I've previously mentioned. The inspections were divided into two separate portions; one based on "Food" and the other called "Standards". The "Food" inspection is exactly what it sounds like, being graded on proper temperatures, dating, first-in first-out rotations and such. Since I had plenty of food-based experience, the "Food" inspection was always a breeze. "Standards" was everything else. Make sure the store is cleaned, employees properly wearing their uniforms, that the shelves were stocked, etc., etc.

"Standards" involved a lot of nit picking. That's not the fault of our inspector, as he was merely following the directives given to him by the company. The bottom of the freezer has a few crumbs, so that's an "X". A customer just bought a 12 pack of cookies we rarely sold, well there's now a hole so that's an "X". The top of machinery no one can see without a ladder looked a little dusty, so there's another "X". Someone changed their mind about their cold beverage and put it back in the wrong spot, one more "X". I really believe this nit picking was intentionally designed to save the company money. As I've already stated, failing these inspections negatively affected the paychecks of the management team.

I've got to say, we were blessed to have a great inspector assigned to our district. He took the time to teach and give pointers on how to pass anything marked with an "X". His willingness to help fed my desire to learn, and I've always been a firm believer in the 'work to learn' model over the 'work to earn'. We didn't pass "Standards" during our first inspection while I was in charge, but it was close. The second time around, the store 'double passed'. Not too shabby for a manager who hasn't been with the company for a half-year.

Before our inspector told us of the "double pass" during his second visit, he stopped to ask me, "How long has Jerome been away on medical leave?"

"Five weeks, Mick."

Mick paced around outside the store for what seemed to be a half an hour after providing my answer, just before giving us the good news of our "double pass". A few days went by after the inspection and Jack finally showed up to the store to congratulate me and the team. Honestly, it felt like it was so long since I've last seen him that I didn't recognize Jack at first. The last time I saw him was my first day on the job.

I addressed my concerns about being the only manager working in the store and asked him if I could at least borrow one of the two shift leads once a week from the bigger Richmond location. "It would nice if I could have an off day." He was reluctant to let me borrow a manager. Instead, he told me I wasn't expected to work every day and to take a day off. Yes, he actually said take "a day" off. I did take a day off, two in fact, over the next few weeks.

After a seven-week absence, Jerome was medically cleared to return to work. There was an adjustment period, relinquishing many of the duties back to Jerome and settling back to the shift leader position. It was a fast and furious learning curve and I was a much stronger shift leader because of it. I wouldn't say it was worth sacrificing the other elements of my life though.

With the relief in my schedule, I was able to refocus on my passions. I eagerly picked up writing again and had more time to spend with my family. While the summer amateur season passed me by, I still had a local professional wrestling career that needed tending. Along with another All-American amateur wrestler named "The Maize Rage" Rampage, we won the Takedown Wrestling Alliance Tag-Team Championships, known collectively as All American Aggression. It was the first time in 13 years I've held a professional wrestling championship, an accomplishment I'm very proud of. I showed off my championship belt at Slowway and a number of wrestling fans went out of their way to shop at our store because of it. The kids loved taking photos with the TWA championship belt.

Rumors were floating around the district I was being considered for a promotion to assistant manager. These were only rumors as I never directly heard it from Jack. My fiancé and Jerome heard these rumors though so there was credibility behind them. The assistant manager position required 50 hours per week instead of the 40 my current position entailed. I wasn't willing to sacrifice my life again and prepared to tell Jack, "Thanks, but no thanks."

Chapter 4

Thanksgiving Eve wasn't the busiest of days, somewhat steady in the morning but a tad slower for a typical Wednesday. Halfway through my shift, a district manager in training came to the store. "Rob, we may need your help in Algonac." He even offered to find coverage for my shift and followed through on his promise. The store looked great, so why not?

"By the way, don't tell anyone," the training DM said as he walked out the door. "That includes your girlfriend. I'll text you when we need you."

Two things crossed my mind. First, she wasn't my girlfriend. I'm going to marry that girl. Second, this sounds like a weird situation. It's not as if I haven't been asked to cover a store before. I've never been told I couldn't tell anyone though.

I received his text but couldn't leave right away as the health board showed up in Richmond. She pointed out a few things but nothing out of compliance. The first time I ever messaged the number associated with our district's cell phone was November 23rd at 10:37am. "I'm on my way. Rob."

"Thanks! See you in 20 or so."

I'm glad they knew how long it took because I'd never before in my life been to the city of Algonac. The city was nestled away in the southeastern corner of St. Clair County. If you weren't going to Algonac, then you've probably never been to Algonac. It wasn't along the way to many other destinations unless you were taking the scenic route along the water, which was a beautiful scene.

While I was trying to find my way I realized, "Damn. They found someone to cover me from the other Richmond store but no one could give me a day off when Jerome was out on medical leave?"

I inevitably found the Slowway in Algonac and parked in the lot across the street, since the Slowway lot was oversaturated. A manger stood outside, quivering as she rapidly choked on her cigarette. Her face was drenched in tears, crying to an older man who was trying to comfort her. I these pair of eyeballs stare me down as they both grew quiet. I pretended not to notice and headed towards the door thinking to myself, "What in the hell am I walking into?"

Near the rear of the building, both district managers were happy to see me. The trainee stood next to my boss as Jack handed me an oversized set of keys. "Congratulations," Jack said. "You're the new general manager of the Algonac store."

Wait, what?

No details were given other than they had to let the previous manager go. I tried to ask a few questions but to no avail. Any logistical answers were, "It's your store, so you can do whatever you want." They were so determined to head out the door.

I stood in the middle of a store with a crew I've never met, in a city I've never been to. Eventually everyone slowly opened up the dialogue, including the random old man consoling what I've learned to be the shift leader, Lonnie. I'm told Len, the recently dismissed general manager of Algonac, was fired for missing cigarettes. The store just had an audit weeks ago, which balances out all of the numbers to get a fresh start from that point forward.

400 packs of cigarettes were missing since the audit. That's over 40 cartons unaccounted for in less than a month. There have been employees terminated for a missing $5 instant scratch off ticket. With nearly $3000 worth of cigarettes missing, in what state of stupor did Len ever believe he wouldn't get fired over something like this?

This would only be the very beginning of Len's problems, but I'll talk about that a little later…

I did what I could, which wasn't much. Of course, I'd introduce myself but I was just buying time. Let me go home and digest everything. I decided I was going to leave after the shift transition, at least giving me the opportunity to chat with 4 of the crew members. And midway through this impromptu store meeting, the power went out.

I'm sure my olive skin turned pale white. "Great." That's a heavily over edited version of my cursive thoughts.

The power outage was a citywide issue. I did what I could, allowing the morning shift to leave and provided some sort of direction to the pair of afternoon employees. "Close down the coffee pots and shut down the grill. Finish today's tasks in the notebook and jump ahead to tomorrow's checklist. There's no telling if it will busy or not on Thanksgiving."

I debated about my new position with the company. I was dead set against taking a promotion, but I wasn't expecting the next step to be a general manager. I was conflicted during the drive home. On one side of the coin, I didn't want to be promoted. On the flip side, if I didn't take it, who would?

The power was still out at 5:53 pm, roughly five hours after the blackout occurred. It started to get dark outside, making it impossible to see anything inside. I needed one employee to stay to open up the store in the event the power came back on. Lonnie, being an Algonac resident and close friend with the employee stuck at the store, volunteered to be there and help. The power finally came back on at 6:46pm.

That was about as helpful as Lonnie would ever be…and now, a little later…

Len being released because of cigarettes was nothing but a reason, and any reason is a good reason. In truth, there was money missing. And I mean a lot of money missing. In a matter of days, I found out through an employee that Len was 'borrowing' money from the store and attempting to pay it back when he received his bonus check. Not that this employee knew exactly what was going on, she just handed me a pair of personal checks made out to Slowway that never made it to the safe. It's a tale I've seen many times before, the struggle of drug addiction. I used to work in the bar scene for over a decade, a job that helped give me time to train for the U.S. Team. But that's another story best told in my upcoming memoir…

Lonnie couldn't see the forest for the trees, as they say. In her world, Len was her best friend who could do no wrong. After a helpful first day, she did what she could to sabotage me. This included telling customers and crew members I didn't know what I was doing. There wasn't any reason for her to undermine me; I hadn't done anything to her. But I'm under the impression Lonnie believed if she could get me fired they would bring Len back. Geez, it wasn't my fault. The two checks I've seen were for a collective $300, so it's not like they were ever going to bring him back.

It wasn't difficult to play Sherlock Holmes and pinpoint Len's drug dealer. Well, I never actually had to play private eye because Jersey openly introduced himself with, "I've got whatever you need, boss." The crew didn't care for him, and I would later find out that in itself was an understatement. While Jersey wasn't crude whenever I was around, I'd hear he acted like he owned the place in my absence. Evidently, this is how he acted near the end of Len's tenure as general manager too.

Throughout my first month as general manager, I've had to deal with the training DM, Jack and Mac preoccupying the office. I've never seen so many papers flying around as they continuously pulled out folder after folder of daily reports. It was the most I'd ever see of my district and regional manager, who questioned the entire crew as they desperately tried to piece together evidence against Len. The one reoccurring theme was Jersey becoming close with Len, and Len lost focus. So my suspicions were sound.

Mac Mooron directed me to bar Jersey from the store. There was previously some legal paperwork sent to his house but it was sent back as undeliverable. "The paper is just a courtesy," Mac explained. "We don't need it to permanently ban him."

I caught Jersey outside, just before he could step into the store. After telling him he was no longer welcome at Slowway, he turned to his friend beside him and said, "It must have something to do with that letter they tried to send me." He saw this coming, so no remorse for his ignorance.

It was an uphill battle with the community, who overwhelmingly didn't want me as the general manager in the Algonac store. I was viewed as an outsider, while Len was a hometown guy who many viewed was wrongfully terminated. I wasn't allowed to talk about any details involving Len's dismissal, there was yet to be criminal charges pressed against him. It didn't help that Len tired to help the community by loaning out packs of cigarettes, something I refused to continue. And every time I told someone they couldn't pay me Tuesday for a pack today, I was the bad guy.

Outside of the store, I was unknowingly being bashed on social media in closed local groups by Len's wife. I eventually got accepted into one of these groups and seen these posts with my own two eyes. I've never met her but she tried her best to discredit my character. After being accepted, I wasn't afraid to put her on blast about it. Instead of responding, all of her posts magically deleted.

Half of the crew aligned themselves with Len and eventually quit. Some gave their notice and finished their scheduled shifts, other did not. One worker in particular was Len's wife's best friend, who I only worked with once. I was in the middle of a gym session, getting ready for an upcoming wrestling show, when I received a text message from the wife's best friend saying she was no longer interested in working for Slowway. I actually had the feeling she was initially going to no-call, no-show. But maybe she realized this wasn't my fault and gave me several hours notice.

We lost enough employees that no one other than me could cover the friend's late-night shift. The shift was a breeze, working alongside two others although one was a nightly volunteer. I stepped outside to enjoy a cigarette when a woman stepped out of her car and asked if we were hiring. She continued to give a sob story about her husband losing his job just before the holidays. I just reached inside and handed her an application. After she left, my two comrades inside looked like they'd seen a ghost. As it turns out, I gave the job application to Len's wife. Whatever, I was smoking the same cigarette after she left so it didn't detract me from anything. Although she made some childish post on social media that must've made her feel better about her odd antics.

My first shop in Algonac was a double fail, which only added fuel to Lonnie's claims that I didn't know what I was doing. Both sections were failed by only a few percentage points and there seemed to be too many simple things marked with an "X". Looking further into these misses and I realized the 'Standards' was failed because too many items were in the wrong place. And with each section of the store that had something stocked in the wrong location was another "X". I'm not stupid. Lonnie was doing this on purpose. It was just another attempt to make me look bad to the higher ups of the company.

As the investigation against Len continued, both of the district managers were still looking for answers. They focused their attention on Lonnie and were obviously gunning for her job. The last day money came up missing was my first day in Algonac and they realized Lonnie tried to help Len cover his tracks. She tried to show them text messages from Len in an effort to save her job, but it didn't excuse her from following his directives after he was terminated. In fact, she showed more than she meant too. The messages surrounding the ones she meant to show pointed to her and Len being much more than just friends.

Another of Lonnie's gripes directed at me was her losing hours. All I did was give her the 40 hours her position entailed without the overtime Len used to schedule for her. She picked up a second part time job and I was willing to work with her schedule. But when I gave her an inch, she tried to take a mile and hijacked the request calendar for the next few months. I actually tried to accommodate her request, but one of them would conflict with my pro wrestling schedule. Request denied. Lonnie bitched up a storm, "I requested to work these shifts." I pointed out she was granted 4 of her 5 requests, and they were only request. She wasn't happy. I heard she was planning a no call, no show and force me to miss my wrestling commitment.

I went to Jack and asked for his permission to schedule Lonnie part time on January 14th. Our crew really couldn't afford it as we never replaced the employees we already lost. Jack didn't want to discuss anything through text. Instead he directed me to talk about Lonnie after our district meeting the following Monday. He basically said changing her availability was grounds to dismiss her since managers needed an open schedule. He asked when we could let her go without disrupting the schedule. I told him January 23rd, which happened to be the first day we rehired an employee that was previously terminated by Len via Lonnie's request.

I found it somewhat humorous when Lonnie saw our newest acquisition to the team. "Didn't we fire you?"

"Yes, Lonnie," I interjected. "And I had it overturned. We need the help."

The three of us worked together for a half-hour before Jack showed up to the store. I wasn't empowered to terminate other manager's, even though she was lower on the food chain. That was

Jack's job. Of course, Lonnie was livid, telling anyone who would listen she was fired because of Len. We even lost more customers due to her accusations. But anyone who inquired was given the same response. "The company gave her a chance. If they wanted to fire her because of Len, they would have let her go when they let him go. She did this to herself."

A few months later, Lonnie apologized to me for the way she went behind my back and tried to sabotage the store. I believe she was genuine with her apology and I hold no grudge with her. It was an awkward time for all of us.

Chapter 5

It was going to take a moment before Jack had a replacement for Lonnie's position. The plan was to transfer a shift leader who was moving to Chesterfield from Ohio. It would be a few weeks before she completed moving, so I just had to sit tight and bide my time while I once again worked every day for the required management coverage. After the timetable passed by, there was no signs of this incoming employee. It took Jack another week before he broke the news, she found another job and no longer interested in working at Slowway.

I brought up to Jack about my concerns about the store lacking another manager, in addition to still being down by 2 crew members. He seemed to come across that it wasn't his top priority until I pointed out that I was making less than minimum wage while being stuck working 70 hours a week on my salary rate. Adjusting for an overtime rate for anything beyond 40 hours, my salary broke down to $8.25 per hour. That was a dollar less than minimum wage in Michigan at the time. This didn't account for any weeks I'd work more than 70 hours if there were any unforeseeable call offs.

I suggested the possibility of transferring one of the two shift leaders at the larger Richmond store, someone who lived closer to Algonac that Richmond. Jack thought it was a great idea and agreed to make a few switches to accommodate our needs and the impending opening in Richmond. However, the timetable was reset and it would be another few weeks before she would join our crew. A long two weeks, but a necessary step back in order to take three leaps forward.

Plans abruptly changed the day before she was set to start. Instead of getting the shift leader from Richmond, I was told we were going to get someone who had previous experience as a general manager for another chain of gas stations in another state. It was tough to make adjustments to the schedule without first meeting her, but that doesn't compare to the hardships Jack placed on the Richmond shift lead. Now she wasn't on anyone's schedule for the next two weeks, as her store already presumed she wouldn't be on their team anymore.

The reason I was given for this sudden switch is this former general manager hinted to Jack she wanted to run a store of her own. Jack tried stroking my ego, something along the lines about having the confidence in me to help train her to become a store manager. If a general manager whose only had the position for a little more than 3 months was the company's best option to train general managers, there are certainly underlying issues this company needs to address.

Jack further told me he didn't plan on keeping me in Algonac, as I was being underutilized if they kept me at that location. It was meant to be a training period and help restore some sort of order after the Len fiasco. While that made more sense, it contradicted the cloud of smoke he blew in my direction earlier in the conversation.

Angel was the person they sent me as our new shift lead and she seemed opened minded during her first day. She had worked at three other locations before making the jump to Algonac. I'd even picked up a few tricks she'd learned at these larger stores, things I was unaware of with my lack of training. It was a helpful few days and I sure appreciated any help I could get to share the managerial duties.

Those few days were as helpful as Angel would ever be…I felt like I've been down this road before…

Angel's first gripe was her schedule. She believed since she was a manager, she should be working the morning shift. While that may be possible in larger stores with more managers, it didn't fit the needs of our outlet. I worked with her, giving her more mornings but some evenings too. I wasn't about to forgo working any mornings. Besides, I liked working various shifts as it gave me a better understanding about my crew's abilities and meeting the needs of the customers. I could never fathom how many general managers thought they were doing such a good job by working only Monday through Friday mornings. There's no way you can ever properly do your job if you aren't working with all members of your crew.

She also thought I was doing too much and couldn't understand why I was focused on so many pointless details. Regardless if I agreed with her or not, I tried to explain the high level of expectations the company had despite not providing enough resources. Angel's constant eye rolls whenever I tried was a telltale sign she didn't believe me. In fact, she didn't think it was her job to do any of the tasks other than doing paperwork. As a manager, she felt she was to direct the crew, not to do "their job". Yeah, so direct the only other worker to do everything?

Angel's issues with the schedule and not completing daily tasks were no excuse to be rude to the customers. She seemed to love the power of a managerial position and enjoyed making it difficult for the consumers. One such occurrence was refusing to let coffee drinkers reuse their Styrofoam cup from earlier in the day. Granted, it was company policy to not allow the customers to reuse their cups but some decisions in a small community such as Algonac needed a bit of discretion. There were only 4 or 5 customers that reused their cups and they came in multiple times throughout the day. Loosing these customers meant we were going to lose over 300 coffee sales per month.

 She also seemed to enjoy making life difficult for the cigarette customers. Slowway had a policy of asking for identification for anyone under 40, and she used that policy every chance she could. Algonac relied on keeping their base of customers happy as we weren't attracting new ones from nearby communities. Customers understood getting carded when a new employee started, but she asked all customers who appeared less than 50 for their I.D. each and every time. I've had so many complaints over this.

 During one such time while we were working together, I noticed Angel reaching for the customer's cigarettes before they approached the counter. She proceeded to ask for identification and I stopped in my tracks to scold her. "If you are grabbing their brand of cigarettes, then you've obviously carded them before." She didn't like my reprimand and took the issue with Jack, who took her side on the matter.

 I started complaining to my fiancé at home about Angel. Come to find out, she was booted from the other Slowway stores because those GM's refused to work with her. I started requesting Jack to bring in another shift leader because I was finished working with her too. All of our sales goals were tanking and the store was in the red on every measurable metric. All I ever received was, "Sorry Rob, but you need to find a way to work with her." Looking back, Jack didn't want to get off his rear-end and find another manager for Algonac.

Perhaps I'm being a tad harsh on Angel's strict enforcement of Slowway's policy of asking for identification. On one particular morning, a semi-regular customer pulled into the lot while I was organizing empty bottles, separating them based on their respective vendors. When I finished the task, I discovered he was a mystery shopper sent by BARS. Angle passed the mystery shop. I'm confident anyone else on the crew would have failed because it was a familiar face that's been carded before. It only reinforced her stance that she was right and I was wrong.

Angel was in for a rude awakening during Mick's monthly shop. As he went through, there were plenty of "X" marks on the most basic of tasks. Again, this was somehow not her job and the high expectations were ridiculous to her. She must've realized she wasn't doing her job when Mick had pointed out so many things not completed. She walked out during the middle of his inspection. We would never again see Angel and I've heard she packed up and moved out of Michigan the very next day.

I did what I could to save face with the local community, turning to social media for assistance. I let it be known Angel no longer worked for us and apologized for the way she treated the customers. I took the blame for the excessive carding, citing we just had a regular customer pose as a mystery shopper. I even explained that we expected more mystery shops as Slowway was about to start selling beer in their Michigan stores. I still had to deal with a lot of complaints through social media, but it worked. Customers started coming back, even those who stopped shopping near the end of Len's tenure as general manager.

We received plenty of compliments, a combination of a cleaner store and an atmosphere that was so much more inviting. The crew hustled to make up for our tanking numbers and we successfully reached most of our goals. The few goals we didn't meet were only missed by a small margin. It was a huge turnaround during the final week of February.

Chapter 6

Jack had to find a replacement shift leader, but it obviously wasn't going to happen anytime soon. For whatever reason, he was now against bringing over the shift leader from Richmond. Perhaps he was agitated at me for being unable to work with Angel. Maybe there just wasn't anyone else available and couldn't find someone to step up in Richmond. It was pretty clear it was going to be much longer than just a few weeks before any solutions were considered.

I wasn't in the same situation as I was in Richmond, where a full staff could provide an opportunity to take a day or two off. So I focused on trying to recruit new employees while Jack figured out a solution to our manager situation. People weren't exactly knocking down our doors with job applications. You had to be at least 18 years old and Slowway offered minimum wage. Sure, you could make a career out of Slowway but it would take several years. I had two employees who've both been with the company for nearly two decades and they both made more than me when my salary was based on 50 hours. It didn't help local fast food locations were offering more money for potential adult employees.

One potential candidate was nice and seemed to have potential, until I realized he had no cash handling skills. His drawer was always short by more than a hundred dollars. I don't believe he was stealing as honest customers would come back during my shift and hand us back the overage he gave them in change. I'm sure not all customers were as honest as others.

Another new hire could never get the concept of promoting the "Slowy Rewards" program, an essential centerpiece to the company's success. Everyone was expected to scan these reward cards 65% of the time. If a customer didn't have a Slowy Rewards card, we were to scan a new card and offer it to the customer. The idea was customers could be hooked by the rewards program, which offered a lot of free incentives compared to card memberships of other businesses, and get them in our stores more frequently. This employee could never reach above 40% within her month of employment. After being talked too and written up for the underperformance on a weekly basis, I had no other choice but to let her go.

These are just a few examples of the struggles in finding quality employees. In the meantime, I've never received any insight on Jack's progression on finding the store a shift leader. Working every day for weeks became working every day for months. I was right back to making less than minimum wage. I would've been better paid with any other position within the company, even being a crew member.

With the summer on the horizon, I fell into a deep depression. I wasn't able to promote myself to any of the regional professional wrestling organizations that caught my attention and now I was faced with being unable to help for another season of the Beach Wresting Series. Finding another job was something I've constantly considered but where was I going to find the time. Some weeks exceeded 80 hours of work. As my world grew dark, I couldn't tell you how many times I just wanted to end it all. Nearly every morning on my coastal drive to work, I gave serious consideration to hitting the gas and running my vehicle into a tree or into Lake Huron. Just so I wouldn't have to endure the punishment of overexerting myself at Slowway any longer.

My saving grace was talking about my feelings instead of allowing it to fester inside my head. I've opened up to my wife and even cried to Mick during his inspections. I hid it from the crew, since I didn't want them to realize their leader was internally falling apart. There didn't seem to be any light at the end of this long, dark tunnel.

I noticed the crew seemed to gravitate towards Mattie, one of those long-term employees I've just previously mentioned. She lived in town and knew the finer details of running the store. In mid-May, I approached Mattie with the possibility of stepping in the shift leader position. She was not up for it, at least at first. I pointed out John's reluctance to find us any help, but that didn't change her mind.

"Mattie, the crew already turns to you. If you don't want to step up, they will eventually send someone who is brand new and doesn't know what they're doing. Do you really want another shift leader like Lonnie or Angel telling you what to do?"

That did the trick as she accepted the shift lead position. She wanted assurance I could work around her other activities, which certainly wasn't a problem. She may not know it, be she might've saved my life. Thank you, "Mattie".

We eventually filled out our holes in the crew. One employee was certainly dedicated but it would take him awhile to get the hang of it. Another pickup was a mystery bag, as one week she would work hard yet the very next week she would do nothing at all. Both were considerable upgrades to the revolving door of other potential candidates.

I did have the chance to compete at the final sand wrestling tournament of the summer, the 2017 State Championships. I even signed up for a mat wrestling tournament before the championships just to have a chance for some practice. It was the first time I'd sign up for a mat-based wrestling tournament in six years, focusing on the sand style exclusively by this point in my twenty-five-year career. Winning wasn't the focus of the mat styles, and I certainly didn't win.

When the action turned to the sand, I made it to the finals of the open-weight adult tournament. My opponent had more than a hundred-pound advantage but I wasn't afraid. Weight classes mean so much more in ground wrestling and sand wrestling focused on stand-up wrestling. The first wrestler to score 10 points was declared the winner with the rules being modified from the international rules. I was quickly down by 8 points after being thrown a few times. I made adjustments and chipped away at my adversary 2 points at a time. Before I knew it, the score was tied 8-8. A bit of controversy with the next score that gave me 2 points for the win, but it could've gone either way. We decided to reset the score back to 8-8 and I won without any doubt to win my second Michigan Beach Wrestling State Championship.

Having a crew and getting back to wrestling helped me climb out of that dark hole, and I was optimistic about what lied ahead.

Chapter 7

Everything was going well in Algonac and sales went through the roof. Our store was number one in the district with beer sales, and second place had less than half our numbers. The team was easily making their selling point goals, even being the number one store in the region in May. Our location was one of the top locations to improve food sales even though we only had a roller grill and thawed out cold sandwiches. Twice the store won a pair of front row tickets for Detroit Tiger games, a monthly award for the top 4 stores improving food sales within the region. Stores weren't allowed to win in consecutive months. If we were, I'm confident we would've won tickets every month.

I tried to convince the higher ups about being allowed to sell more items for our grill, pointing to our leap in sales. Slowway had a structure to follow with request and I had to get permission through the marketing department. It took marketing 3 months to tell us "no" on selling egg rolls and another flavor of tornadoes. The reason given was there were only so many resources and these items were being saved for the higher volume stores. I felt it was a big contradiction towards the focus on getting a larger share of the food market. My fiancé helped me transfer egg rolls though, even without anyone's permission.

Much of the community was aware of my involvement with wrestling. I handed a copy of *Hosting Beach Wrestling Events* to the local wrestling team and they started hosting an annual tournament called "Sand Wrestling in the Swamp". I sold tickets and hung up flyers for the Blue Water Championship Wrestling shows in Port Huron, a longtime professional wrestling organization I've been fortunate to be a part of since they first started after the turn of the millennium. I used an article from the July 6th issue of the *Times Herald* newspaper as an icebreaker to customers, being pictured on the insert located on top of the front page of the issue. The article wasn't about me, but it was nice to be tagged along in the featured story of a local standout by the name of Kef Sweat (later repackaged as "Aquabruh" Cyrus Satin).

The residents of Algonac overwhelmingly made me feel welcomed at my home away from home. For the most part, I'd engage in small talk with just about everyone. I'd discuss entertainment psychology on a daily basis with a local daredevil act by the name of Genghis John, the Human Firecracker, who wore a protective suit covered with firecrackers for an explosive show. I'd even had another wrestling fan sell me his collection of WWF Hasbro figures at a reasonable price, reinvigorating my interest in the collection (as well as the newly released "retro figure" series modeled after that Hasbro line of figures). I could go on with many other memorable conversations, but I don't want to veer too far off the road with my Slowway story.

Mattie quickly progressed as the store's official second in command, she was a natural. I watched her confidence skyrocket as the months flew by. Jack hinted in the past he wasn't interested in keeping me in Algonac for the long haul, and he reinforced this belief as Mattie continued to develop. She was clearly one of the top managers on his list of being promoted to general manager and the timetable given was the end of 2017. His projected timeline was bumped up after another general manger decided to step down from the general manager position at one of the stores in Fraser.

"Do you think Mattie is ready to become a general manager," Jack asked.

"Give her a little bit of time to get on her feet, but yeah, she will do a great job."

"Are there any suggestions about someone becoming the shift leader?"

"I have been working with someone," I answered, referring to the rehire that caught Lonnie by surprise earlier in the year. "But it's no longer my call to make. You should ask your new general manager."

So the decision was official. I was going to take over the store in Fraser within a few weeks of the conversation I had with Jack. The move sent me from the northeastern most store in his district to the southwestern most location. This gave me a bit of time to benchmark the Fraser store and get an idea on the location, layout, and meeting my new crew incognito.

And my walk was going to be an uphill battle. The store was in complete disarray. Too many things were missing from the shelves, the coolers were as bare as Old Mother Hubbard's cupboard, and the store was filthy. This "janitorial dream" wasn't worth the extra $50 a week I was given for taking on a higher-level store, but I saw it as an opportunity to prove the worth of this penny.

My final day working in Algonac was heartbreaking. The crew became a second family to me. I'd be closer to my wife's store; we officially tied the knot during the summer. She ran the other Fraser location just a half-mile down the road. I thought it would great to be closer to her, and maybe offer her some help as we were expecting a little bundle of joy within the next few months.

Chapter 8

I took a long weekend before officially taking over the GM position in Fraser. I got to witness my longtime friend, Andrew D'Arcy, accomplish his lifelong goal. Ever since I've first met Andrew, he has always talked about his desire to host a professional wrestling event at McMorran Arena in Port Huron. It was the home of minor league hockey and has also hosted concerts, the circus, and Broadway shows.

This BWCW show featured a 'meet and greet' with the legendary Hall of Fame wrestler, Road Warrior Animal, along with a slew of standout regional talent. It was an honor to be included on the show. I teamed up with BWCW's most popular wrestler, "Mr. Fitness" Slim Trimmons, a fitness instructor who believed in the nutritional value of the Twinkie. We were collectively called "Twinkie Power" and I still team with Slim to this day at BWCW shows. Twinkie Power helped reinvigorate my wrestling persona after I've grown a bit stale from a solo run designed for this former BWCW Cruiserweight Champion to put over newer wrestlers.

I came into Fraser determined to turn the store around as quickly as possible. I'd overhear a few employees and customer say things such as, "If he doesn't slow down, he's going to give himself a stroke." I'm sure my crew didn't know what to make of their new general manager because I've changed a lot of the rules. I over ordered product with the thought, "If we don't have it, we can't sell it." I no longer allowed anyone to pull food products too early, wait until after lunch to pull any food set to expire later in the day instead of pulling them first thing in the morning.

Paperwork was never my top priority, and I forbid allowing my managers to do the paperwork until after 9am, after the morning rush.

I did say managers in the plural sense. Unlike Richmond and Algonac, I was blessed to have two shift leaders instead of one. This greatly reduced any chance I would be stuck working every day without another manger. Both had their unique set of strengths and weaknesses but I was confident in their set of strengths. The rest of the crew was strong as well, except for a flakey part time overnighter who quit not long after my arrival. I led by example and witnessed everyone around me up their game as well. Within two weeks after I started working in Fraser, Mick came in for the monthly inspection and we double passed with flying colors.

The double passed caught all of the higher ups by surprise. According to Jack, the store hasn't double passed in over 10 years. There's no telling how long it's actually been as no one could pull up any reports beyond 10 years. Mac came out to congratulate me and the crew, even hinting I was ready for a bigger store. We would double pass two more times before the end of the year. We failed 'Standards' in October because cleaning products weren't allowed to be visible to the customers in the bathrooms. Having a brand new, never before used cleaning brush was enough to automatically fail. We were just one cleaning brush away from double passing each of the final 4 months of the year.

Maybe a little over a month after arriving at Fraser, I had an odd request from the higher ups. They wanted to know if I was still in the system at the Chesterfield store and if I had any passwords to the computers. I laughed it off with an astounding,

"No. I haven't been there in over a year." I could tell something major happened but wasn't keyed in on anything.

As details started to make its way around the wire, Maggie walked out of the store. As the story goes, she's been struggling in a few aspects and repeatedly asked Jack for help. Jack was either unwilling or unable to help and Maggie put in her 2-week notice. Just a day or two after her notice, she needed his help again and he refused to answer his phone when she called. This just prompted her to toss the keys at one of her crew members as she walked out the door. Within the next few days, the entire store quit except for 3 employees. By all means, this is just hearsay on my part.

My wife and I were atop the initial list of possible replacements. My wife has done an amazing job turning around a store that was rumored to be closing before she took it over, as her store never turned a profit before she became the general manager. My ability to turn a store around quickly put me right behind her on the list of candidates. Since my wife was about to go on medical leave to have our baby, she was scratched off their list. And since I just turned around a store that's been underperforming for the past 10 years, they didn't want to move me just a month after being placed in Fraser. They eventually found another general manager from another district to take over the Chesterfield location, which was a good move for the new GM. I'd heard it was much closer to home for her.

As well as I was doing in Fraser, it didn't reflect in our Light Product-Break Even (LPBE) rating, a measurement that trumped all other measurements to senior management. In fact, it had a much higher bearing on the managerial bonuses than the Mick's shops did. At first, I couldn't understand what I we were doing wrong. This equation was a measurement on how much money a store made or lost per gallon of gasoline sold. Anything better than 3.5 cents of profit was considered great. In Algonac, we averaged 20 cents of profit per gallon sold during the summer, which was outstanding. The LPBE equation is this…

(Inside sales-operation costs)/gallons sold.

If you're good at reading numbers, then you can already see where I'm going with this but allow me to elaborate for clarity purposes. This equation is not a measurement for the profitability of a store. While we sold more items from the inside, we also sold more gas so our LPBE looked bad.

The LPBE could be positively manipulated by strongly encouraging the gas-only customers to shop somewhere else. You can look like a rock star by telling customers to hit the road. In what other industry does that business model work? It was just another tool for the company not to pay their employees what they're worth.

Issues like the LPBE just gave me incentive to figure out strategies for the store. I wasn't going to focus too heavily on logistics at the moment; we were expecting a baby and bought a new house. But I started making notes for the upcoming symposium, a meeting for all of the general managers within the region.

Chapter 9

I looked forward to January as I was set to get my first performance-based raise from the company. Jack and I talked about it near the end of December and he seemed genuinely impressed with my performance throughout the year. He even let me know Mattie and I did an amazing job in Algonac, as the store was so profitable it was designated as a higher-level store. Jack was just waiting for my review to officially cross his desk.

Instead, Jack delivered some bad news. Because I took a promotion to a higher-level store and took a raise, the calendar was reset for my performance review. I wasn't eligible for a raise until September.

I was upset but I didn't hold it against Jack. I was just a casualty based on a technicality within the company's policies. I let it fester at home and started to realize not only would I have received my performance raise if I stayed in Algonac, but I would've also got a bump for the store being on the same level tier as Fraser. In a nutshell, I'd be making more money if I would've stayed in Algonac instead of agreeing to take on a more difficult store.

While being discouraged on feeling screwed over on my rate of pay, I discussed the issue with a few close members of the Fraser crew. I discovered our longest tenured employee wasn't making as much as the two long term employees in Algonac. It wasn't even close, despite the 3 of them have been with the company for just as long. I brought up being underpaid and underappreciated to Jack, not only for myself but my Fraser employee too. He came back with a generic, "Well, if we give you two a raise then everyone else is going to want a raise." His excuse was crap. As much as I was displeased with my own situation, I was more upset I couldn't successfully fight on behalf of my employee.

It became just another topic to add on my ever-growing list for the symposium.

I've never been to one of the company's symposiums before, and I liked to joke that is sounded something like a carnival which included a concert. It was nothing like that. In reality, it was a just a boring region-wide meeting with the purpose of the general managers being informed about the future direction of the company. The running theme was Slowway trying to rebrand themselves as a fast food establishment instead of a gas station. They were going to remodel stores to include an in-house restaurant and improve food selections at the stores that weren't going to be remodeled. They believed so much in this endeavor, the company was going to invest 6 billion dollars on the project.

There was some positive news from the symposium. There was going to be incentive for the gas-only customers to make inside purchases by earning discounts at the pump. There was an idea of lessoning the cost of the selling point candy in the morning hours, when customers were less likely to want any sugary treats. There was also a restructuring of the in-store managerial structure, giving new positions and a raise for some of these titles.

Before I give the company too much credit for the positives, the wage increase for assistant managers was equal to what many other retailers were offering as a starting wage for crew members. This was an attempt to retain managers. In order to do so, some managers were sort of being demoted. In my store, one shift leader was going to be promoted to assistant manager while the other remained a shift leader. They stripped away the bonus potential for the shift leaders, which meant they're going to make less money but expected to do the same work. My shift leader quit as she was essentially making $50 less a week. Many other shift leaders who didn't get promoted to assistant manager also severed ties with Slowway.

Another questionable decision was to increase the amount of transactions before technically needing another employee on duty. The amount was raised considerably, 65 transactions per hour before needing a second employee, more than 130 to meet the new requirements in order to have a third. It was another poor decision made by people who have never actually worked inside the stores. My mannerisms surely spoke volumes to the higher ups, as they could easily see my displeasure among these and other decisions I believed to be a bad idea. It was difficult to hide while I'm seated in the front row.

My antics drew the attention of Mac, who came directly to me following the conclusion of the meeting. "I'm glad you made it here, Rob."

"We didn't talk about anything we should have discussed today," I replied, pointing to my sheets of prepared notes.

"Well, we only have so much time."

"Mac, we didn't discuss anything we should've been."

Later that week, our store was forced to start ordering plastic carry out bags of inferior quality in an effort to save some pennies. I'm sure it looked like a sound decision on paper, but there was nothing but problems. Anything that needed a bag now required 2 bags. Any purchases that used to require 2 bags now needed 3 or 4. So in addition to increasing the transaction count for more authorized hours, transactions were intentionally slowed down. As a result, stores were no longer staffed to meet customer demand. We hardly had enough hours before these conflicting decisions.

These bags were so poorly manufactured that 1 out of 10 rolls needed to be thrown away right out of the box, as one side was open on every bag. The cheap presentation caused some customers to shop elsewhere and others to minimize their purchases. The new bags were also more difficult to open. For someone like me who had preexisting issues with my hands and wrist, this was creating health issues and prevented me from doing my job.

I brought my concerns to Jack and asked him about any reasonable accommodations. He assured me he would look into it but I didn't believe him. I repeated my deteriorating health conditions to him over and over again, just to feel dismissed. After sounding like a squawking parrot for so long, I addressed my concerns to Mac.

He replied via email on March 19th. The email said the following, word for word…besides the alterations to hide their true identities…

"Rob, Jack and I have discussed and we both want to make sure your concerns and request below are addressed in a timely manner. Jack will stop by tomorrow to discuss with you further. Thanks, Mac."

When Jack came in the two mornings later, there wasn't any mention of my accommodation request. There was no concern either. Jack was livid I brought the issue up to Mac. He did seem to calm down near the end of the conversation, but he certainly shown his true colors. I pinned all my hopes on Mac following through on my request. I tried to put it out of my mind for a while, since I've already learned request take some time to accommodate. It took marketing 3 months to tell me I wasn't allowed to sell egg rolls in Algonac. For months afterwards, I could sense Jack was still resentful I went over his head by bringing this up to Mac even though he did his best to hide it.

Just 3 days later, my hands completely shut down. I went to the clinic and was given a note excusing me from work for the next two days. I even found coverage for my next shifts and sent the note to Jack. The following day, our fulltime overnighter was in a horrible automobile accident and needed time off to heal. My crew was already thinned and I was initially unable to find coverage. I messaged Jack to see if I could cover these overnight shifts despite being instructed by a doctor not to.

"You can not work if doctor says no. It a liability for the company." The misspellings are present in his March 23rd response.

I started taking it easy when I returned to work, only scheduling myself for 40-hour weeks. I would burn up vacation time to compensate for the 10 hours I was missing. I also started scheduling my employees beyond the hours authorized to the store. While it was meant to make my job a little easier while I awaited a response from Mac, it helped increase sales. On average, the schedule was 30 hours over per week. But according to another measurable program, our store was either fully staffed or understaffed. It never said we were overstaffed.

Opening up my schedule gave me the chance to help the Beach Wrestling Series in the summer. I haven't been around the style of sand wrestling for a few years and wanted to get reacquainted with a sport I will forever hold dear to my heart. I made the decision to sign up for the 2018 Beach Wrestling National Championships in North Carolina. I wasn't in the shape I was in back in 2011, the last time I've competed on a national or international level. I wasn't sure how well my hands would hold up either.

Competing was only a small reason for going. I wanted to start hosting tournaments again and update *Hosting Beach Wrestling Events* to reflect any rule changes I might've missed. I also wanted to gauge the potential of hosting a Beach Nationals in the future, as I felt if we held just one it would greatly improve the Michigan summer series and open the door for other Great Lake states to embrace this international style.

While I had a great time, I wasn't even close to earning a spot on the 2018 U.S. Team. I did earn a pair of All-American honors, one for the veterans division (sometimes joked as the "old man" division amongst the wrestling community) and another for the style of 'belt wrestling'. I was really intrigued by learning about sand modified belt wrestling, even though my first match was a loss to the defending World Champion. It's a style I felt would complement sand wrestling exceptionally well, and there's a U.S. Team for belt wrestling too.

I've seen some old faces and met some people I've had conversations with for the very first time. I only wished I would've brought my family with me, not that I stayed long anyhow. Carolina Beach is a beautiful area with plenty of activities. I fully intend to visit again, even without the incentive of a national level wrestling tournament.

Chapter 10

It took a while for many of our vendors to adjust to my over ordering ways, but they let me know we were going through just as much product as the stores on Hall Road. I was excited by the news as the trio of Hall Road stores were considered to be the jewels of Jack's district. Sales were up in every measurable aspect and I found out the company was doing what was called a "cooler kickback". The incentive to buy multiple items from the cooler to earn discounts at the pump was successful and the company realized for many stores, the coolers were too small. They were authorizing reconstruction to expand the size of the coolers.

I kept pushing food sales with the idea if we made the list of stores set for a "cooler kickback", maybe we could convince them to include a "food kickback" too. Jack and the crew seemed to love the idea. Jack had some concerns, such as outdoor space to meet such request. I simply pointed to an empty house owned by the church beside us which was being used as a glorified storage shed. We wouldn't have to buy much property and my proposal wouldn't interfere with the operations of the church. I even mentioned to Jack the pastor was regular in our store and once brought over the church choir to sing for us as they were all treated with frozen beverages.

I wanted to raise the level of this location. The focus on the food and the cooler was the centerpiece of my plan with the hopes of the kickback concept. I pointed out there wasn't any fast food location within a mile radius of the store and if the focus was on food then the company was missing a golden opportunity with this location. I started to believe we didn't have any competition, except for other Slowways competing with the company's limited amount of resources.

If we raise the store to another level, then my rate of pay would fix itself.

I didn't account for my hands failing more frequently. I also didn't account for not hearing back from Mac after 3 months had gone by. I started contacting him again but only this time I'd never get a response.

Many times, my hands failed during my days off. Other times, I would do what I could which included working one-handed. The only way I could open coffee packets was with the aid of my teeth. My assistant understood and did what he could to help cover portions of my shift, but he also had upcoming personal commitments. Many members of my crew tried to help and the customers could see I was hurting and seemed to understand. Not that I didn't keep trying though. If I could just make it to the end of the summer to keep our numbers up during the busiest part of the year, I'd take a medical leave and try to find solutions to my health problems. I even hired an extra person to account for my upcoming leave of absence.

As much as I tried, I couldn't make it to the end of the summer. On one particular shift, my hands were in such bad shape that I couldn't do anything except ring up orders and process credit and debit cards. I couldn't make coffee. I couldn't do paperwork. I couldn't even handle cash or hand customers their receipt. Literally, all I could do is ring up orders and run their card. Even then, I kept trying. Jack was fully aware of my ongoing issues and allowed me to continue working hurt.

In the wee hours of Saturday, August 11th, I woke up to my hands not functioning properly. I sent a text message to Jack at 2:50am to let him know. I offered to work that day with such short notice but told him I needed to take my leave of absence and asked him to find coverage for my remaining shifts. I also let him know that both my assistant and the long-term employee were out on vacation, so anyone within my crew wasn't really an option.

Jack called the store after the lunch rush and asked how I was feeling. There were only a few hours remaining in my shift and I assured him I could make it through the end of my day. He asked me to send him a copy of a doctor's note along with my passwords for the computer, the safe, and other various equipment requiring passwords. He assured me he would find someone to cover my shifts. And I followed up on his request, sending him the doctor's note and my passwords at 4:05 pm.

My next shift was for the following day from 5am-1pm. I received a call from my overnighter at 5:20am asking where I was. I told him Jack said he would have my shift covered and drove to the store. I tried to call Jack but he never answered. Having already been told I wasn't allowed in the store when a doctor excused me from work, I felt trapped in a corner. I was obviously going to lose my job if I stayed, not that I could do anything anyways. I did the only thing I could do and secured the store, asking the overnighter to close down the grill and the coffee pots before locking the doors and shutting off the pumps before I left.

Well, I did one other thing before leaving. I felt slighted and wanted to bring this to the attention to the highest of higher ups, the president of the company. I outlined what has been happening to me over the past 5 months. I explained how Jack wasn't helpful and how I'd never heard back from Mac about any accommodations. I wasn't hiding my email from Jack and Mac, blatantly including them in this email.

My health was so bad I needed to go to the emergency room later that day. I called human resources on Monday morning and requested to be placed on immediate medical leave. I was asked to get clearance from my district manager and told them about yesterday's situation instead. There was going to be an investigation over the weekend events. I received a phone call from Jack on Tuesday at 12:04pm telling me I was no longer employed with the company. I've heard he's tried to tell everyone I walked out. Funny, I didn't know you could walk out of a job when I wasn't allowed to be there in the first place. He never mentions he said he would find coverage or anything about the doctor notes, which at the time of my termination I've been medically excused by 3 different healthcare professionals. To save his job, he claimed he never received my messages or talked to me, despite stating otherwise before I talked to HR that Monday morning.

It's not as it Mac and the president of the company wasn't aware of my ongoing situation, fully aware I was medically excused from August 11th through August 23rd, the day I was scheduled to see a specialist. They allowed for my termination. They fully endorsed discriminatory practices in doing so.

I'd like to think my stats spoke for themselves. I helped raised a store to another level and on pace to do it twice is just as many years. My team between 2 stores has reached their selling point goals for 17 consecutive months, a streak only ended by my termination; only 8 stores reached their goals in December out of 103 stores. My team was number 1 in May of 2017 and while I've never seen an official list for June of 2018, we beat that May mark by a 12% increase. We crushed our food goals by over 1,000 units during my final full month and set to shatter that metric by 2,500 the month I was let go. I'd like to think I've proved myself as a strong asset for the company.

    Jack has only paid attention to his Hall Road jewels, which is only 25% of his district. He has demonstrated a pattern of leaving his general managers helpless whenever they need him. I'd like to think he's proven himself to be a liability for the company. Yet Slowway chose to retain a liability while dismissing an asset.

    It would take me 3 weeks to heal enough to return to work, and I still had issues with my dominate hand that needed a total of 10 weeks of downtime. At least I finally sought the medical attention I needed. It wasn't hard to find another job and had 3 job prospects offering me more money after I healed, one of which would've been a $4 an hour raise. I turned that offer down as I didn't want to return to retail and settled on one of the other two offers. One bummer is being asked about my interest level on being a member of the 2018 U.S. Team after my termination, an offer I had to regrettably turn away since I was hurt and broke. But it's only a step back for this tarnished penny. A step I know will give me the chance to make three leaps forward.

Chapter 11

Just like the preface, this eleventh chapter is added content to the original *Corporate Lunacy* story. It's been 9 months since the release of *Corporate Lunacy*, so I've had time to reflect on the aftermath of my story.

A major concern was my Fraser crew. Everyone worked hard to help the growth of our location. They were my extended family. When Jack pulled his 'no-call, no-show', forcing me to secure the store, my assistant manager and senior-most employee were on vacation. I was worried upper management would try to strip away their rightfully earned time off. They didn't mess with the senior employee. I wish I could say the same for my assistant manager.

The store was already short-staffed. Jack believed he could strongarm my assistant, who unfortunately was scheduled to work the day following the store's closure. He made a comment in front of 3 managers, each from a different Slowway store. "The assistant manager just bought a new car, so he needs this job. He will have to give up his vacation." The assistant manager didn't buy a new car, he had his car painted a different color.

The assistant manager didn't budge and willing to quit if his long-requested vacation wasn't honored. He told Jack, "The only reason I even agreed to work one day during my vacation is so Rob didn't have to work every day." The company allowed him to enjoy the rest of his time off.

The statement Jack made in front of the 3 managers quickly spread throughout his district. His lack of empathy for the in-store employees was exposed. He lied to his General Manager's about my termination, in which my crew and my wife let it be known I had a doctor's note and Jack authorized my excused absence. He lost all respect from the employees within his district.

Jack struggled to fill the General Manager vacancy. My wife and assistant manager were willing to step in, but Jack wasn't willing to let either of them take the position. I'm sure my assistant's unwillingness to sacrifice his personal life for the better of the company was the strike against him, because he was certainly qualified. My wife was supposed to take over a bigger store on Hall Road, a request that came from Jack's boss, Mac. A General Manager was retiring, and part of the reassignment plan included my wife's promotion. She had consistently performed near the top of every measurable metric in the region over the previous 2 years.

After being denied the ability to take over my former store, "Well, I'm not going to Hall Road. The only way I could've been transferred was because Rob was working in Fraser. Our kids go to school in Fraser. Since you guys fired him, I can't leave my store."

No one else within Jack's district wanted to be the General Manager for my store. Mac had to step in and find someone from outside of Jack's district to take the GM position. They also had to go outside Jack's district to find a new GM for Hall Road.

I filed plenty of complaints against Slowway, winning most of them but also losing a few. The company paid half of my wage for my final week, even though I was fired 6 days into the pay-week. They were forced to recognize my absences excused by doctor's, and had to use my "sick pay" benefits during those absences prior to my termination. Providing proof that Jack authorized covering my shift also helped my case. I lost my claim for backpay during my time in Algonac, when I was forced to work 70+ hours a week for 13 weeks. I may have won my claim, as companies cannot use a salary as an excuse to curtail minimum wage laws, but I failed to make this claim within a year after it happened. It was dismissed due to statute of limitations.

My unemployment claim is an interesting final story to share with you. Slowway contested my unemployment claim with, "Rob didn't provide a 2-hour notice as required by the operations manual". I provided the unemployment agency with proof I had contacted Jack 3 times prior to the shift, with as much as a 26-hour notice. When presented with my documentation, the company didn't offer any type of rebuttal. I won 3 weeks of unemployment benefits with a generic response about the company not proving an adequate reason I should be denied benefits.

About 2 months later, I received a letter of re-determination from the unemployment agency. I was unaware Slowway appealed the original decision, as the unemployment agency never asked me for any additional information. The company maintained their position, "Rob didn't provide at least a 2-hour notice," despite documentation to the contrary. This time, the determination was not generalized. "You properly notified your employer about your absence and your last offense was due to a personal illness over which you had no control. Misconduct in connection with work has not been established."

While I felt vindicated with the determination, I knew Slowway would appeal again, which they did. The next stage of the unemployment claim was over the telephone with a judge.

Surprisingly, Slowway only sent Jack as their representative. Mac, the Human Resources representative, and the president of the company all played a part in my termination, yet none of them were willing to join Jack to fight my claim.

How did the phone call go? I posted about it on social media, so it may be best to simply share the post with you. There are slight modifications to provide clarity and fix spelling errors.

"I just want to rant...

I won my initial unemployment claim from my previous employer...and won the 1st appeal too. The 1st determination was a generic response, but the appeal win was nice. It explicitly stated my termination was in no way my fault. But it didn't end, as there was another appeal. One in which me, my former supervisor, and a judge were all on a conference call...man-o-man, I wish someone else from "Slowway" was on the line...

Either way, I've been waiting for this moment...to get "Jack" on the line...it may be the closest I'll ever get to a face to face confrontation.

Knowing the case was being pleaded to a judge, you'd think my former supervisor would have been a little prepared. The very 1st question to him was my hire date and role...both of which he got wrong. So wrong, in fact, he told the judge my hire date was my termination date...the judge called him out on that. Even then, he just made a date up despite it being stated on the paperwork provided by "Slowway".

That was just the beginning...he screwed up so many times I can't remember then all...

Thankfully, he didn't deny being provided with a Dr's note or saying he would have my shift covered (which he didn't follow through on; instead rolling over on me with corporate on why the store was closed). Instead, his silly claim was I was supposed to send it HR. Thankfully, the judge grilled him, treating him like an idiot.

Funny thing, he cited my outgoing email to the CEO of the company, claiming I quit in that email...

"No, that was a whistleblowing email. I felt it was important that he knew his district and regional mangers weren't doing their jobs."

That's about the only moment I could get that jab in, and he shut his mouth for the rest of the conversation. Ultimately, I won the 2nd appeal too...another determination saying my termination was in no way my fault.

Usually, this is the stage "Slowway" no longer pursues fighting unemployment claims...but not too many employees write a book calling them out on their plethora of bottlenecks.

I expect another appeal. Looking forward to it."

     I was actually surprised Slowway did not appeal this decision.

     As far as I'm concerned, the issues I've had with the company are resolved...at least the best they ever will be. I'm not going to dwell about them anymore. I'm sure I've spent far more time thinking of them than they will ever think of me. How do I feel about these 4 in the aftermath?

     Looking back, I don't have any hard feelings towards the CEO of Slowway. He was obviously lied to by everyone involved, and their 3 voices silenced mine. I believe he's allowed Jack to keep his job, despite evidence clearly demonstrating Jack failed to do his job. This may slightly tarnish the CEO's legacy within the company, but it's his right to do as he pleases with his reputation.

I also don't have any hard feelings towards Mac, the Regional Manager. He was also lied to by Jack, being assured my issues were addressed when they really weren't. While I don't blame him in that regard, he kept silent when the issue was brought to his attention again. Maybe he didn't know how to respond without admitting the company was in violation of federal law. Mac was quickly transferred to an emerging market elsewhere, and I'm under the impression he wasn't given a choice about uprooting his family to another state.

There wouldn't have been a story for you to read if our Human Resources representative had done her job, as I would probably still be with Slowway. She failed to investigate my claims. No one from my crew was questioned until after *Corporate Lunacy* was released. She failed to keep her word and follow up with me for more testimony and documentation. If she had done any of these things, I would have kept my job and Jack would have been terminated. In the end, I'd like to thank her for not doing her job. Otherwise my wife and I wouldn't be working elsewhere, as we both found better paying jobs with less than half the hassle.

Before I get into how I feel about Jack, let's take a look at my medical accommodation request he submitted on my behalf. After all, he's told me and my crew the request was "Still being looked into" every week, for the duration of 6 months. Flipping through my personal file, there's memo made out by Jack. This doesn't appear to be anything official, but rather something jotted down on a piece of scrap paper.

It reads…

"On 3/16/18 Rob sent an e-mail to RM stating he is working too many hours, his pay is poor and he is working hurt. On 3/19, I went to talk about this with him and he was off. The next day I tracked him down and spoke of these issues. He stated the injury was old. He lied to me. He stated his hours and money he came up with was not his actual pay but he felt the average dollar per hour he worked. An over or untrue statement as I looked up the money on SAP. I asked him why he went around my back; he stated he thought Marcus could grant him more hours and/or give him a raise as he already approached me about it. Rob has threatened quitting before or making false statements and when confronted he recants saying "he was stressed out, and need to let off tension". I told him this has to stop. If this continues additional discipline will take place up to and including termination."

This was apparently my accommodation request. Obviously, my biggest mistake was having any faith in my district manager. I certainly learned Jack's memory is horrible (I mentioned wages long before being hurt), he has trouble tracking down his GM's when they are working at their assigned stores, and he isn't very strong with basic mathematics. While this memo is certainly slanted to place me in a bad light, he actually put in writing he was fully aware of my preexisting injury. It's so slanted and scrambled, this should have been a red-flag to whomever this was sent to.

So how do I feel today about "Jack Dickenwetter"? You've read the response to my accommodation request. I've turned over several documents from medical healthcare professionals to Jack, none of which were inside my company file. While I understand he may have been upset I brought the matter to Mac, I did so only after coming to Jack first. He allowed me to continue to work hurt and watched with his own eyes how my health was deteriorating without any accommodations. I will forever resent Jack. As far as I'm concerned, he maliciously tried to strip away my ability to hold my baby daughter. I will never forgive him for that.

I'm in a much better place today, although I still feel the effects of being forced to work hurt at Slowway. I have a much better work-life balance, giving me time to write, be involved with wrestling, and spend more time with my family. I wasn't bothered about not being able to be a part of the 2018 U.S. Wrestling Team, although it turned out to be the final year national teams were sent for the Beach Wrestling World Championships. Now there is a series of international tournaments, and a point system is used to determine the World Champion in each weight class.

I wasn't allowed to wrestle professionally for 10 weeks while I gave my arms a chance to heal, but had a few no-contact roles on a few shows during that timeframe. As I write this, I still team up with "Mr. Fitness" Slim Trimmons as the team of Twinkie Power, and we won the 2018 BWCW "Tag-Team of the Year" award. I also still team with "The Maize Rage" Rampage as All American Aggression, finally losing our TWA Tag-Team Championships after a 910-day reign with the titles. I've since been cast as a "Commissioner" for MPWA (based in southeastern Michigan), and I'm having fun learning a non-athlete role while also gaining experience as a play-by-play commentator.

All in all, my time at Slowway was only one very small segment of my life. It's time to finally 'let it go', as my wife often tells me. If you know me, you may already know what type of rollercoaster life I've lived, which is far more interesting than this memoir. I'm willing to share these stories with you, with a targeted release date for *A Solid Performance* being set by mid-2022.

Made in the USA
Lexington, KY
22 August 2019